OPTIONS

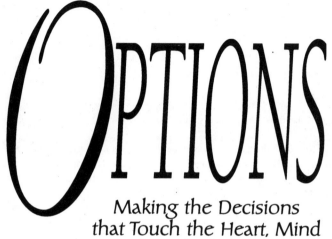

OPTIONS

Making the Decisions that Touch the Heart, Mind and Soul of a Woman

Karla Gottry
A Very Personal True Story
as Told to Her Husband Steven

Priority Multimedia Group, Inc.
Mesa, Arizona

Distributed by:
Macalester Park Publishing Company
Minneapolis, Minnesota

DEDICATION

To Maisie, Michelle and Kalla, and any other women — younger or older — who still have so many decisions to face in their futures.

ACKNOWLEDGMENTS

Thanks to my mom and dad, for understanding and caring, and for still being there...in spite of myself. You both worked so hard to make a better life for your daughters..."thank you."

Thanks to Kathy and Konnie, for loving and accepting their sister who seems to have gone through about everything imaginable.

Thanks to Kalla Paige, for bringing so much joy into my life everyday. I love you and your hugs so much!

Thanks to Steven, my husband, for listening to the whole story and loving me anyway. Thanks for giving me the encouragement to do the book, and for putting my thoughts into words. I could not and would not have done this without you.

Thanks to Mark Darling, of Evergreen Community Church, for leading me to this...and to Tracy and the Drama Team for seeing it through.

Thanks to God, who gives the greatest gift of all — life — so that any and all of us can live beyond our mistakes, if we but trust and believe in His Gift to all of us — Jesus Christ.

And thanks to you, my readers, for understanding that my feelings, opinions, experiences, and beliefs may be different than yours — yet they're as real to me as yours are to you. I hope and trust that what I am sharing will be of value to you.

CONTENTS

INTRODUCTION

Right at this very moment, there's a kind of war going on. People are fighting, and protesting, and maybe even shooting each other, over a big question that is on the news every day. And that question is, "Do you, as a pregnant woman, have the right to choose whether or not to have that baby?"

The answer, according to the laws of our nation right now, is, "Yes, you do." You have the choice. You can have the baby. Or you can have an abortion, and put an end to the uncertainty of the future.

But what you need to know — what nobody may have ever told you — is that you have other choices. Other options. More choices about your future, and the future of the baby growing inside you. You need to know that your decisions today will affect your tomorrow.

This book is about the many choices you can make. It's about the many options you have. It's about the options that I had and where my decisions led me, because they became the experiences of my life. After you read this book, the choices you make are all yours.

I just want you to know two things. I'm not going to tell you what to do. And I'm not going to judge you for the deci-

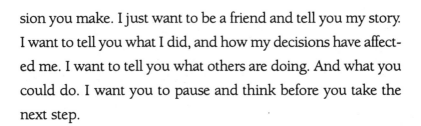

sion you make. I just want to be a friend and tell you my story. I want to tell you what I did, and how my decisions have affected me. I want to tell you what others are doing. And what you could do. I want you to pause and think before you take the next step.

This whole thing isn't about protests and picket lines and TV news cameras. This is about you. And only you. Because no matter what path you decide to follow, it will touch your life.

With Love,
Karla Gottry

The Past

I, Karla Gottry, small town girl from Minnesota, have had an abortion. There, I said it. You don't have to wait until the end of this book to find out if I'm among the millions of women who have made the same decision.

But you have to know that it wasn't easy for me to admit this fact in the first sentence of the first chapter of a book.

You see, no woman I know wears a little badge that says "I've had an abortion," or even "I gave my baby up for adoption." These things are private, and we all try to keep them that way.

So, why this book? Why am I willing to share my story if

this is such a private, personal matter?

Let me answer by telling you some of the things that this book is *not*.

First, it's not about telling you what to do. You have the choice, under the laws of this land, to do what you believe is best for you.

It's not about changing the laws that grant you the freedom of choice. We elect lawmakers to make, change, or improve upon laws.

It's not about marches and rallies, either for or against choice.

And it most certainly is not about burning or bombing Planned Parenthood clinics or murdering doctors who perform abortions. I have no time for people who do that. It's completely illegal and immoral.

So this is not a political book. Nor is it a "Here's what you should do if you ever find yourself pregnant when you don't want to be" book.

This book is, and is nothing more than, a story about love — how I sought it, found it, lost it, misunderstood it, and finally — experienced it. How I lost my first love, became involved in an abusive relationship, faced and dealt with an unplanned pregnancy, and, after much uncertainty, found certain love.

I am not a special person with an unusual or unique story. In fact, you may even see a part of yourself, or someone you care about, in the pages that follow.

I grew up in a wonderful home filled with all of those great "traditional" family values. (What an overused expression *that* has become!)

My dad worked hard, driving trucks — sometimes seven days a week, often well into the night. My mom was a hard-working homemaker, making life as good as she could for her husband and three daughters. We went to church every week, and we loved and honored and respected each other.

I was the middle daughter, two years younger than Kathy, and five years older than Konnie, the "baby." For me, this meant more than a few hand-me-down clothes, and, of course, a few battles for my position in the household. I quickly learned how to use the system to my advantage. I played by all the rules — or at least gave the impression that I did. I was involved in Camp Fire Girls and church activities. Life was pretty good, in spite of our family's lack of money during my growing years.

Then, something happened. Something wonderful! I met

a guy. I first noticed him in the hallway at school, standing by his locker. His name was Gary.

Everything about him appealed to me. He was a year older than I was, and a year ahead of me in school. I liked that! He had a great physique, and a husky, low voice. He was into motorcycles, and loved to party. In fact, his nickname was "Animal."

Do you remember your first love? The intensity of the emotions that you had never experienced before? The "can't wait to see you" feelings? My heart was experiencing things I didn't understand. And I loved it!

Almost instantly, Gary and I became inseparable. During the school day, we would grasp any time we could find to be together — even the brief minutes between classes. I'd spot him coming down the hall, and my heart would jump, my pulse

would race, and a smile would overtake me. I could see in his eyes and feel in his touch that he was experiencing the same intensity.

When we couldn't be together, we would talk for hours on the phone. It was the next best thing. We only had one phone in the house — I had to speak softly so my parents and sisters wouldn't overhear our conversations. "Karla, get off the phone!" became the most frequently used phrase in our little house. "You've got two minutes," Dad would shout.

It didn't take long to discover that Gary and I had much in common. We weren't part of the "in crowd," and didn't wear all the right clothes. We found our own group to hang out with — other kids who were pretty much like we were. One of our friends would offer to drive us around for hours in his car, just so we could sit in the back seat and make out. Yet Gary respected me, and never once tried to push me to have sex with him.

We both came from working class families, but we were filled with dreams. So we both held down jobs in order to get some of the extra things we wanted. Gary would often stop by the restaurant where I worked and order a Coke, just so we could see each other. In between customers, we'd plan our next time together.

But there was so much more to Gary than motorcycles and parties and an appealing appearance. He had a heart that was bigger than any I had ever known. Our gang used to joke that he was the only person we knew who would brake for a snake. He was the one who made sure we included our handicapped friend in all of our parties and school events. He gave people a helping hand no matter who they were. It was how he was raised.

He was also raised to love his country. One night at a party held near the end of his senior year, Gary made an announcement that stunned me.

"I'm enlisting in the Marines."

I looked at him for the longest moment, unwilling to believe a word of what I had heard.

"Why?" I finally demanded. "Why would you?"

"Because it's my duty," he simply said.

"You can't go! I won't let you!"

The thoughts that were racing through my mind were the memories of friends who had died because of duty and honor and all those other patriotic words and feelings. Our small town had been hit especially hard by the tragedies of war, and those who died were friends of mine.

I didn't bring up the subject, though. I was too terrified. It was the most intense time of the Vietnam era. Thousands of men — or boys — Gary's age were coming back from "that awful place in Asia" in body bags. Some weren't coming back at all, left to decay in an overgrown jungle or in a muddy rice paddy.

When Gary made up his mind about something, it was settled. The next day we drove together to the Federal Building in Minneapolis. He had to take a physical and sign some papers. I remember thinking "I hope they find some little thing wrong with him — flat feet, maybe — so that he can't go."

They didn't.

As Gary's graduation approached, my emotions took control of me. I cried myself to sleep more than one night. I was angry at the war that had called him to serve. I was afraid — for Gary, for me, for our love for each other. How could I ever live without him?

The night before he was to board a bus and head off to boot camp, I did something I never planned. I pushed every feeling of guilt out of my mind. I took Gary's hand and led him up a narrow flight of stairs to a friend's bedroom. We were alone. We shut out the sounds of the party going on downstairs. And we made love for the first time. His first time. My first time. It was my way of bonding our love, of keeping thoughts of him ever close while he was so far away. I was able to prove to him that I could give myself to him completely.

The next day, Gary left. There was nothing I could do about it. So I cried.

— — —

It didn't take long for the mailbox to replace the telephone as the most important thing in my life. I wrote to him every day. First to boot camp. Then to a large base in California. During every class of my senior year, I would think about the letter waiting for me at home. That was about the only thought on my mind. I couldn't wait to tear open the envelope and somehow become closer to him.

There was never any question what I was going to do after graduation.

"I'm moving to California so that I can be close to Gary," I announced one night at the dinner table.

"You are NOT," both my parents said, almost in perfect unison.

"You're too young. You're still only seventeen. We won't allow it."

"Too, bad, because I'm going," I screamed.

And so the battle began — a battle that consumed my last year of high school. I was determined to win. I had to be near Gary.

The day after commencement exercises, I was on a west-bound plane headed for Los Angeles, with all my worldly possessions packed in the two suitcases I had received from my parents as a graduation gift. I moved into a beach house with my older sister, Kathy, and three of her friends.

I had left home that day — the home that had for so long

been filled with love — without ever resolving the conflict with my parents. Looking back, it's something I would never do again. We all have choices we can make in our daily lives. Going out of our way to heal wounds should always be the choice we make. But I didn't know any better.

Gary was stationed at Twenty-Nine Palms, just a three-hour drive into the desert. He hitch-hiked into the beach cities every weekend to see me. It was wonderful! At last we were free to be together more often! We enjoyed every moment. And we talked about getting married. Then, even if he was sent to Vietnam, I'd be closer to him, back in the states, making wonderful plans for our life together.

First, though, we'd have to save for a ring. Nothing big, but at least a gold band with a small diamond. We took turns opening our billfolds and placing all of our money on the table. Between us, we came up with $43.00. It was a start!

Gary never had to go to Vietnam. And we never got to pick out the ring.

— — —

It was my first Christmas in California – my first Christmas away from my parents. Kathy and I wanted to go back to Minnesota to be with our family, but we couldn't afford the airline tickets. So we spent those lonely holidays with others who had no families nearby.

Gary, however, got a military pass and flew home to see his parents. He volunteered to carry our presents for the family with him, and then bring their gifts to us when he returned the day after New Year's.

I was waiting at the airport when his flight came in. I was so eager to see him. There would be just a little time together before his next flight back to the Marine base. But a little time was better than none at all.

When he got off the plane, we hugged and kissed for an embarrassingly long time. Actually, I wasn't embarrassed, and neither was he, but the other passengers probably were. We walked arm in arm to the baggage claim area, and were confronted by a minor disappointment. His bags were missing. We checked with the airline and eventually learned that they had been sent to Palm Springs by mistake. So with only his carry-on, Gary said good-bye and boarded the plane. "I'll see you on the weekend," he called back to me.

I watched until the plane had disappeared completely from

view, and then walked to the parking lot with tears filling my eyes. "I miss him so much already," I thought. "But at least I'll see him in a few days."

The rest of the evening was gentle and uneventful. I watched some TV, did my nails, and picked up a book that didn't hold my interest. All the while, I thought of Gary. I dreamed of the future.

It was very early in the morning when the phone rang. "Who could be calling now?" Kathy answered. It was Dad.

"Is Karla there with you?" were his first words.

"Karla? Sure, she's here. We were asleep. Why? What's wrong?"

Suddenly, Kathy became very quiet. Then she started shaking. "Karla, it's for you," was all she said. She could barely speak.

My life, my dreams, my plans, were destroyed the moment I picked up the phone. "What is it, Dad?"

"Karla, it's about Gary. There's been a terrible car accident. The highway patrol called his parents. They called us right away because they thought you would be with him." Dad's voice was trembling.

"Is he okay?"

"We don't know how bad he is. We just know he's been taken to the March Air Force Base hospital."

I didn't even allow myself the thought that Gary could die. "He'll be fine, he'll be fine. I've just got to get to the hospital. I've got to be at his side."

Kathy knew I was in no condition to drive by myself, and she was terribly upset, too. As I threw on my prettiest dress —

I wanted to look my best for Gary — she called another friend, also a Marine, and asked him to drive us to the hospital.

The drive lasted a couple of lifetimes. The thoughts that filled my mind now became dark and negative — and then hopeful and positive. "He's going to die. No, he's going to be fine. What will I ever do without him? Wait — we're going to have beautiful children together." But why, then, did I keep seeing him in a casket every time I closed my eyes?

As we raced toward the hospital, it suddenly occurred to me that I had left my sunglasses behind.

"I've got to stop at a store," I panicked. "I need to buy sunglasses. I've been crying. Gary can't see me like this."

"Here, take mine," Kathy volunteered.

We arrived at the hospital and parked in the first open spot

we could find. By now, there was only one thought on my mind. Gary. Nothing mattered but Gary.

I was told by the nurse in the intensive care unit that I was the only one authorized by Gary's parents to go into his room. I was to be the representative of the family, because his parents couldn't come up with the money to fly out to California to be with him. I'd have to face this all alone.

"Oh, God," I cried when I first saw him. "OH, GOD!" But I wasn't sure God heard me. I stood there, frozen, at his bedside. I could barely look at him. His head was totally wrapped in long bandages, and blood was still oozing from the back of his skull. He was hooked up to every kind of life support I could imagine. I knew he would never make it. But I had my hopes, my dreams, my love. He was too young to die. Wasn't he?

I wanted to know what had happened, and learned all the details from one of the others in the car. Gary had hitched a ride with three other servicemen in order to pick up his bags in Palm Springs. The driver, for whatever reason, made a sudden, screeching stop. Gary was riding in the back seat, the car flipped, and he was thrown through the back window and onto the pavement. Gary and the driver were the only ones taken to the hospital. The other two walked away from the accident.

So I sat there next to his bed, day after endless day. On the third or fourth day, I'm not sure which, the doctor decided to confront me with the awful truth.

"If your friend lives — and we're not sure of that — he'll never be anything more than a vegetable. We've already removed part of his brain."

I couldn't speak. I was stunned into silence.

Then it hit me. It didn't really matter if Gary couldn't walk or talk or hold me again. "I love him. I'm here for him," I said. I believed that when you're in love, you're committed.

I stayed at his side those long days and even longer nights. Never hearing him speak. Never seeing his eyes open. Never sensing any kind of response. So I just touched him. I talked to him. I kissed him. Still nothing. Did he know I was there? Could he sense my presence? Could he hear me? Could he feel me?

Then, exactly one week later to the hour, without ever having said a word to me — without ever even saying good-bye — Gary died. And I cried. And I cried, "OH, GOD!"

The Search

I stood by the open grave, that frigid January day in Minnesota, never hearing one word the minister said. I was numb. People were afraid to approach me. They didn't know what to say, and thought that I would suddenly break down and lash out at them.

Never once had my dad ever cried in front of me. But he did that day, as he held me, protecting me as best he could from the cold wind intruding on our lives. I felt sorry for my mom — Dad always held her in the cold.

She cried that day, too.

Just before they lowered the casket into that dark, cold hole in the ground, I placed a red rose on its glistening surface and made my final vows. "Gary," I spoke softly, "I will love you forever, and I will never love anyone like I love you."

— — —

After the service, the funeral director came over to me, put his arm around me, and tried to comfort me. "You're going to be okay. It'll be all right."

Liar! As much as I appreciated his efforts — he was the one person who dared to approach me — I knew it wouldn't be all right. This was my one love. My only love. My life.

The days went by in a blur of pain and apprehension. My parents were afraid to leave me alone, for fear that I might do something drastic. As unconscious as I was throughout all of this, I managed to notice that I had missed my period. "Oh,

God," I said, "I'm pregnant with Gary's child. Thank you, God."

I was excited and frightened at the same time. But the thought of ending the pregnancy never entered my mind. A child would be the perfect way to hang onto a piece of the man I loved. I could raise a "little Gary." Our child would be visible and lasting evidence of our love for each other. I would have something.

It turned out to be a false alarm. I slipped into a deep depression. No Gary. And now, no part of Gary to cling to.

I never returned to Los Angeles after the funeral. I never cleaned out my desk at the office. Kathy had to pack my belongings and ship them back to Minnesota. I moved in with Gary's sister in Minneapolis and tried to let the healing begin.

Each passing day simply passed. I hoped the days would

become a little less painful, but they didn't.

I finally decided that getting back to work might help make the days shorter and keep my mind occupied. I knew the nights would still be long. I had a recurring dream — that I was falling, falling long, falling fast, and Gary stood at the bottom of the abyss and shouted, "NO, KARLA!"

It didn't take me very long to find a job, and it also didn't take me long to attract the attentions of another young man. His name was Pat, and he was as kind and tender as anyone I had ever met. From the beginning, I spent most of my time with him talking about Gary, and he listened patiently. We became good friends and close companions.

When he asked me to marry him, I pushed my pain into the darkest corner of my mind that I could find, and said "Yes."

I thought Pat would be the perfect companion, yet all the while, I could still love Gary. We had a beautiful church wedding. Just before my dad walked me down the aisle, he jokingly whispered, "Are you sure you want to do this, Karla?" Dad and I both cried a little that day, but my forced smile told everyone that all was right in my world.

No fault of Pat's, it obviously wasn't. My heart still belonged to Gary, so I was unable and unwilling to give myself to my new husband. I loved him as a brother, but nothing more. The words still echoed: "Gary, I will love you forever, and I will never love anyone like I love you." They must have been true.

I realized that, with Pat, I could have all the things I wanted out of life. A nice house in the suburbs. A fancy car. New furniture. Dinner parties. Beautifully decorated holidays with

my family. But what would all that really mean? In time, I talked less and less. I began to retreat into a shell. I was hurting so deep inside.

When our isolation from each other became too much to bear, we mutually agreed to a divorce — something I never thought would happen in my life.

We made a pretty silly sight at the lawyer's office. I was sitting in Pat's lap with my arm around him. We were both crying. The lawyer asked, "Are you sure you want to get a divorce?" But there was little other choice. Emotionally...mentally...I just could not be married. To this day, Pat has a very special place in my heart. But "brotherly love" cannot hold a marriage together.

After Pat and I split up, I moved back to Los Angeles, back into another house near the ocean with my sister...again. Kathy always accommodated me with an open heart. Both of my sisters are like that.

I began dating again, too, because it was the thing to do. "After all," I reasoned, "I deserve a nice dinner out once in a while." Yet I couldn't feel anything for the men I met.

Finally, at the urging of my friends, I agreed to seek professional counseling. I recognized that I somehow had to bury Gary and my dreams. Thinking that my sessions with the counselor had resolved my deeper issues, I felt I was better able to confront life where I had left off. One day, without warning, my "Fairy Tale Prince" appeared on my doorstep. His name was Jim.

Jim had the wonderful ability to treat a woman like a princess! He held the door for me, bought flowers, and put me on a

pedestal. He treated me in ways that are considered old-fashioned by many women today, and I loved it!

It soon seemed right that I should marry again, so Jim and I planned our wedding — my second church ceremony, but much smaller than the first. I didn't even invite my parents, because I was embarrassed about getting married for a second time.

Our wedding day was my last wonderful day with him. Like Jeckyl and Hyde, Jim turned into a monster, right before my eyes. His anger festered to the surface, and he took it out on me in brutal and merciless ways. The police were summoned to our home more than once. He was insanely jealous, and would scream foul names at me for coming home an hour late from shopping. And I just took it. Perhaps I was just getting too tired.

The verbal abuse gave way to physical abuse. He began to throw things at me. One morning, I dodged an entire set of coffee cups, some filled with scalding hot coffee. Another night he threw me out into the yard in my nightgown and locked the door. If he didn't like something I said or did, he would grab my arm, force it behind my back, and pin me against the wall. As time went on, he started to abuse my two dogs. He would hurt them in front of me, because he knew how much I loved them. Somehow, I could tolerate what he did to me, but not to my dogs.

It was a humiliating and degrading existence. I think of it now as a slow crucifixion. Yet I was determined to stay married to him, because I didn't want to admit to having made another mistake. I didn't want my parents to know. Protecting my family was...and is...very important to me.

People in abusive relationships tend to hang onto that one little glimmer of hope — that one tiny sign of change. The truth is, you can't change the abuser. Maybe counseling can help. Maybe the only hope is prayer.

But you have to be alive to pray.

That's why, one night in late November, I changed my mind. I had no other choice. It was live or die. Jim was a hurting, lonely human being. His soul was empty inside, and he was terrified of losing me. It was that fear that drove me away, and he couldn't even see it.

That terrible night, I climbed into bed beside him, just as a wife should. Without any warning. he drew out a loaded handgun, pulled the hammer back, pressed the cold steel against

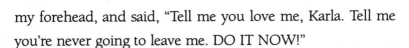

my forehead, and said, "Tell me you love me, Karla. Tell me you're never going to leave me. DO IT NOW!"

The verbal abuse was unbelievable. He kept taunting me. "Tell, me you love me, Karla." I did exactly as he asked. I told him that I loved him with all my heart. "OH, GOD!" I pleaded in my mind as I lied to my husband, the man with the gun. "OH, GOD, PLEASE HELP ME!" But I was sure no one was listening.

Crying out "Oh, God" had somehow become a habit with me. It was just something I said when the situation had become seemingly hopeless. And each time, my cry came from deeper within me. My soul, too, was so empty.

I hated emptiness.

The Aloneness

The next morning, without Jim's knowledge, I was on the first flight to Minneapolis. My job in the sales office for a large airline made it easy for me to get on a plane almost anytime I wanted. I hurriedly arranged an interview with another airline, got a job in their Twin Cities sales office, and planned my immediate move.

I knew Jim would respond to my decision with angry words, violence, or worse; so I returned to L.A. and simply played the game his way for a couple of weeks while I made my plans. But I was absolutely terrified every moment I was in that house — every time I saw him walk through the door.

Driven by fear...and a strong desire to remain alive...I left behind most of my furniture and household items, and secretly had the movers pack just a few things. To avoid a drawn-out court battle, I let Jim have our house. Money was the least of my concerns.

During that very difficult time, I faced another tough decision. If you're an animal lover, you'll know what I mean.

I was running for my life, and I had to act quickly. I knew I couldn't take both of my dogs with me, so I had to choose. It was a cold decision made at a critical time. I chose the smaller one who was also younger. He would live.

Then I bought some hamburger, and cooked the best "last meal" I could for my older dog. I sat on the floor next to him, and cried as he ate. Every few seconds he'd look up at me, and

I was sure I saw sadness in his eyes. Maybe his instincts told him what was about to happen. "I hope there's no pain," I thought. "I hope he can forgive me."

I put on his leash, and still crying, drove him to the veterinarian's office.

The receptionist asked me why I was there. It was difficult for me to speak, and I whispered through my tears, "I have to put my dog to sleep."

She captured my sense of urgency, as the others in the waiting area tried to listen to our conversation. She called the doctor immediately.

All of the people waiting in the reception area somehow knew that I had no other options. Without judging me – without asking what had brought me to this painful decision – they

simply hugged me, cried with me, and supported me.

The doctor asked me if I wanted to stay with my dog as he "drifted off to sleep."

"No, I don't," I bawled. "I love him too much."

I felt like adding, "I've lost so much of what I've loved." But I didn't. The doctor didn't need to hear my story.

"Do you want his leash?"

"No."

And I simply ran out.

My first few months back in Minnesota were painfully lonely. I rented a small room in a house owned by an elderly woman, and pretty much stayed to myself. I forced myself to scrimp and save, often stretching a single package of hot dogs and buns

into meals for a week.

When I had saved enough money, I put together a down payment for a small townhouse in a sleepy little suburb of Saint Paul. The day I moved in, I felt as though I was truly home at last! Starting over!

Little did I know that when I was outside working in my small garden, or washing my car, or simply enjoying the sunshine, I was being watched!

His name was Tom, and he was a charming, handsome executive who lived directly across the street. He walked over, introduced himself, and quickly informed me that he, too, was alone — and in the midst of a divorce.

He charmed me on sunset walks, he charmed me in fine restaurants, he charmed me during candlelit dinners at his place, and he charmed me into the bedroom.

I hadn't been held in a man's arms in so long. I hadn't been told that I was a wonderful person in so long. I was so alone. It all felt and sounded so good. I didn't say a word. I was being swept away into a world I hadn't experienced in far too long.

I thought I had taken every precaution, because the last thing I wanted to do was get pregnant. I knew I could never deal with THAT.

At dinner a few weeks later, I noticed that Tom was staring at me with an odd look on his face. "There's something different about you tonight, Karla. You have sort of a glow. I think you're pregnant."

"No, I'm not," I protested.

"Wouldn't hurt to check, you know," he concluded.

Just my luck. A visit to the doctor's office confirmed what Tom had already suspected. I was going to become a mother. My mouth dropped. "I can't be pregnant," I thought. "It's simply not an option."

The nurses gathered around me, all excited. I asked if I could see the doctor. When he saw the look on my face, he knew I was not ready to have a baby. So he looked in his book, wrote an address on a slip of paper, and handed it to me.

I called Tom at work to tell him the news. His response caught me completely off guard. Very softly, he whispered, "I love you."

"But what are we going to do?" I asked.

"Come home," was all he said.

When I got home, he came right over. There was a seri-

ous look on his face, and his first words were, "I guess we'd better talk." I sat down, wondering what he was thinking about all of this.

"Karla, this is the last thing either of us needs right now," he began.

"So what are you saying, Tom?" I interrupted. I thought maybe this was going to be his exit from my life. I asked him directly, "Are you saying you don't want to get married?"

He hesitated. "I'm not even out of my first marriage yet, Karla. And I have *my* daughter to think about."

"Should I end it?" I didn't use the word abortion. I didn't like that word. It sounded too cold, too calculating, although the phrase "end it" isn't much warmer.

Tom remained silent for the longest time.

"So? So?" I prodded.

More silence.

"If we're not getting married, I don't have any choice, do I, Tom?"

It was obvious that he didn't want this to be his decision. His silence forced it all on me. Again I was faced with tough choices. Again I felt so terribly alone. It gave me a chill.

"I'll help you through it," he finally said. "And I'll pay."

I took out the slip of paper the doctor had given me, and made the appointment. Tom volunteered to drive me to the clinic, and said he'd be there to take me home after it was all over. Go in, get it done, come home. Just a simple thing. Hardly know it's happening.

I experienced that old feeling again. I didn't know if I had

the energy to make this decision — much less have a baby.

"If I can just get this over with, I can get on with my life."

Queen of Denial.

The Moment

After I signed some legal-looking forms, I was led into a small private room and instructed by the nurse to push the "Play" button on a VCR. I was supposed to watch a video that would tell me what was about to happen. Seemed simple enough. Necessary enough. But I had blinders on. I wandered all the way through this...without ever thinking...without ever even wanting to think.

I didn't hear a word of the video. I was — for yet another time in my life — completely numb. I think they said something about a "procedure" and "minimal discomfort," and "take it easy and rest for the next three days to prevent bleeding."

Never one word about any other options I might have. Never one word about my apprehension. My fear. The guilt I was feeling. Or what I'd experience and feel in the days, months, and years ahead.

I discovered something. At least I thought about it later. Once you've arrived at the clinic, you're pretty much committed. This is *going* to happen to you. Their reason for *being* is to end your pregnancy — not to help you work through the issues. After all, if you were to walk out, they wouldn't make any money on you. I didn't know that. Maybe no one who walks into this does.

In retrospect, I wish someone had told me about the other choices any pregnant woman has. We don't necessarily have *all* of the choices, but we do have *some* of them. Could someone have snapped me out of it? I don't know. I was pretty far gone.

The nurse returned, told me to put on a hospital gown, and lie down on the table. She said that the doctor would be in to see me in a few minutes. I think she sensed I was frightened, because just before she left the room, she said, "It'll all be over soon. You'll be fine. It's no big deal. Women do this every day."

"Not me," I thought. "I don't do this every day. If my mom and dad knew where I was right now — and why — it would break their hearts." I couldn't even bear to think about it. It was breaking *my* heart. My dream had always been to fall in love, get married, and raise a family. I had fallen in love with Gary, buried him, married a nice man who was more like a brother, divorced him, married a man who could have killed me as easily as not, fled from him, met another guy, got pregnant...and here I was. "When will I ever make a good decision? When will things ever go right for me?" I turned these questions over and over in my mind as I waited for Doctor X to come into the room. To this day, I still don't remember his name. It might really be "X" for all I know.

The doctor seemed to be very cold and matter-of-fact. I think that to him, I was just the next body in the next room, waiting for him to get rid of my "problem."

"Since you're in your first trimester, this is actually rather simple and straightforward. We're going to use this suction catheter to extract the tissue from the wall of your uterus. It will be relatively painless, very quick, and your recovery time will be minimal."

"What a popular word 'minimal' has become," I thought. Minimal time, minimal pain, minimal tissue, minimal recovery. Oh, yes, they forgot one: minimal relationship.

They didn't tell me the truth about the pain. I'm not sure whether it was purely physical. Or mental. Or emotional. Or maybe even just simply imaginary.

No matter what. To me, it was very real, whatever kind of pain it was.

I laid back, put my feet in those awful stainless-steel stirrups, stared at the tiles on the ceiling, and tensed up. As the doctor inserted the suction device, I thought I would be relieved of my tension, guilt, pain, and uncertainty in an instant. Quick as a flash of lightning. Done and over with. "Hurry up, please."

I've heard that for many women, that's the way it is. It may be true for you, or for someone you know. If so, you don't have to believe one word of what I'm going to say next.

For me, it was a moment of excruciating horror — worse than anything I could ever imagine. At the moment this unwanted "tissue," this inconvenient baby-to-be was sucked out of my womb, I honestly knew that something far more significant was happening. Suddenly everything came to a virtual standstill, and it all happened in slow motion. It was as though a living spirit was leaving my body. A spirit I had birthed at that moment — even though it had not been born in the flesh.

I was overcome with sounds and feelings that are almost too complex to explain. It was as if this living being inside me had not simply left. It had escaped. I sensed a glorious sound

— the wind, perhaps. Yes, that's it! The spirit escaped in the wind. And, in that moment, I connected with my baby's spirit as it left my presence. Then, I crashed down into a well of silence. Emptiness. Stillness. Pain.

No physical pain I had experienced to that day — or have experienced in the days since then — could equal what I felt at that moment. I have no doubt that there was an actual human being growing in me. This was my baby, and I had chosen to end its life. I knew in an instant that I had made the most tragic decision ever.

All I could do was cry out, "Oh, God." But I knew He could never hear anyone who had done what I had just done. He could never hear me.

The Loss

I don't *know* for certain. There's no way I could ever know. All that was removed from me was tissue. With little hands. Little feet. A little beating heart. A little brain that was too young to comprehend what was happening.

But I do *think* my baby was a little girl. I always wanted to buy pretty little dresses, and tie a cute ponytail, and go to school programs and sit in the front row at dance recitals so that I could take pictures.

These were dreams that would have to wait.

That day, in that clinic, I lost the chance to experience a child being born, to hear the words, "It's a girl!" To nurse her, to watch her grow, crawl, and walk. Talk, learn, sing and dance. To go to the prom, graduate, get a career, and someday walk down the aisle at her own wedding. To have her own children — my grandchildren. It still hurts when I realize what my decision cost my own mother — her grandmother.

But that's not all I lost. I lost Tom, a man I thought loved me enough to marry me and stand by my side and raise our child. Tom eventually went back to his wife — for a short time — and then moved on to bigger and better and younger things. I often wondered what it was about me that didn't fit with his dreams. He's married again, and has moved to another state.

If I had allowed my daughter to be born, I know the approximate date she would have celebrated her birthday. So every year, on that date, I think about her. Every year I think about a darker day, too. I think about the day she left me, and the thing that hurts the most is that I was the one to say good-bye.

"Oh, God," I would whisper every time I got that awful feeling again.

Then I'd think about choices. About the options I had, but ignored. I know an 18-year-old girl named Michelle. She became pregnant by a guy who didn't give marriage a second thought. He immediately suggested an abortion.

She said, "No, I won't do that, but I *will* give the child up for adoption. Then I'll go on with my life."

She made careful plans and arranged for the adoption to take place right in the hospital. But when her daughter was born, the baby suddenly became very sick. The doctors told Michelle that the only way her child would survive were if she were to get nutrients and antibodies from her. Nursing her was the only way to build her immune system.

She cared enough about this young life to do what she had to do. She nursed her, comforted her, held her, and stayed up long nights with her.

Then, when she was well enough to turn over to her adoptive parents, Michelle changed her mind.

She could have said, "Here she is. Take care of her, love her, be her mommy and daddy." And that would have been fine. Giving a child up for adoption because you can't take care of him or her is a noble, loving, and self-sacrificing act.

But something special had happened. She had bonded with her baby. She had fallen in love with a child who needed her and loved her.

Michelle is still single. She works hard to provide a life for herself and her daughter. It's a battle. There are more bills than money. There are colds, flu and injuries to deal with. There may even be some fear of the future.

But through some miracle, she still has her child. I don't. The pain of my loss is very real. Very lasting.

The Alienation

After I went though the abortion, I thought I had lost everything any woman possibly could.

I had lost Gary, the love I thought I could never replace.

I had lost two marriages — one as a result of the graveside pledge I had made to Gary, the other to an unwillingness to be injured or maybe killed in an abusive relationship.

I had lost a child, and the father of that child.

There was nothing more to lose, I thought.

I was so wrong.

Without even thinking it was possible, I had suddenly lost the truth. My integrity. My self respect. Out of seemingly nowhere,

I instantly had this "big secret." A deep, dark secret I couldn't share with anyone.

Remember how I said that no woman I know wears a little badge that says "I've had an abortion," or even "I gave my baby up for adoption." I said that these things are private, and we all try to keep them that way.

Well, it's true. The first people I had to protect were my parents. They'd be heartbroken if they found out that their daughter had gone through an abortion. They could never find out. What would their friends think? When I was growing up, one of the biggest concerns was "What would the neighbors think?"

Then, there were my own friends. I had friends who marched in pro-choice parades and attended pro-choice rallies, but I couldn't even tell them. After all, not one of them had ever admit-

ted to having an abortion.

How about my "husband of the future?" How could I ever fall in love and face the prospect of telling him what I had done? He might think that the procedure had somehow ruined my "insides" and that I could never have his child. He might think I was impure, or not worthy of his love.

The big one, though — the scariest one for me — was God. I knew little about Him, but I was sure He wouldn't approve. If the abortion wasn't enough to do it, then He was sitting up there on some cloud ready to stomp on me the next time I made another mistake. And I was, it seemed, on a roll.

I was, in a word, alienated. Alienated from my parents, my friends, any man I would ever meet — and God.

"Oh God," I asked. "What next?"

Reconciliation

When I started dating Steven, my first thought was, "Don't tell him anything about your past. He'll walk for sure."

But as I gradually got to know him, I learned to trust him, and I saw him as a person who could forgive and move on with things. He told me about some of the disappointments and setbacks that had happened to him in his business and career, and how he had discovered the power of forgiveness and reconciliation.

We developed a wonderful relationship and a deep love for each other. We enjoyed so many of the same things, from dining out to boating, from quiet walks to tail-gating at a foot-

ball game. We both love to travel, so we often dreamed of the places we wanted to see together someday — Hawaii, the Caribbean, Italy, Greece, Japan. We even attended church together. That's the way we were brought up.

I was anxious to start over — I looked forward to the future. It seems I never give up hope.

When we began to discuss the possibility of marriage, I decided I'd better let it all out.

"There's something I have to tell you," I began, "and I don't think you're going to like it." He looked at me, and without saying a word, encouraged me to continue.

"I have a whole boat load of baggage in my life"

"We all do," he said.

I told him about Gary, my vows to him, about Pat and Jim.

"And, I...I...I've had an abortion."

"And...?"

"And I haven't wanted to tell you because I thought you could never accept that in your wife."

"You weren't my wife at the time, though," he replied.

"I know, but I don't want you to think I'm casual about these things."

"Is it something you'd do again?"

I was sure of my answer. "No, never. Never again. The pain was too deep. And I'm not just talking about the physical pain. I'm talking about the emotional pain. I miss my child. It hurts."

I started crying, and Steven held me.

"It will heal someday," he said softly. "And it doesn't change my feelings for you."

"Oh, God, thank you, God," I prayed silently. And I began to think that He just might be listening.

The Joy of Healing

We got married in front of just a few friends at the church we had been attending. During most of the service, I found myself thinking and praying, "I hope I finally got it *right* this time."

After the ceremony, we treated our friends to dinner at a private club where he was a member. The next day we boarded a plane for San Francisco, and had the most beautiful honeymoon I could ever have imagined. We laughed, we talked, we loved, we shared, we gave ourselves to each other completely.

Every honeymoon, though, comes to an end. Even the good ones. Upon our return, we immediately became immersed in our daily lives. Steven owned a successful advertising agency,

and had managed to acquire more toys than I thought were possible — a boat, an airplane, a Mercedes, a convertible sports car, and even his own limousine. Maintaining it all was practically a full-time job.

As time went on, he poured more and more energy into his business. I spent more time than I wanted to in my new sales position. Then, too, we had clients to entertain on the boat, business trips to take, and vacations to plan. It didn't take long before we noticed that we were too tired to get up for church on Sunday mornings.

"No big deal," we rationalized. "God knows where our hearts are."

I'm certain He did know, too. They weren't with Him, that's for sure.

All my life I'd talked to Him, called out to Him, never knowing if He heard me. Now I didn't even talk to Him.

Before we got married, we worked long and hard to resolve another major issue. Steven had two children from a previous marriage and wasn't interested in having babies around the house. I wanted a second chance at having a child. I truly felt cheated.

To resolve this issue, we sought the wise counsel of a pastor Steven knew. (See how I'm finally catching onto this? If you need help, seek it out. Don't try to handle everything on your own.)

Pastor Al's advice included these words, "If you decide to have a baby, just hope and pray that the minute Steven looks into the baby's eyes, he falls in love. Otherwise, you don't have

a chance."

We had been married almost four years when I got pregnant. I was both thrilled and terrified. "What will the days and months ahead be like?" I wondered. "Will Steven accept another child with open arms, or will he grow to resent me for wanting to have a baby?"

Because I was being true to myself for a change, I had to take that chance.

My pregnancy was uneventful, and I was grateful. I wish I could say the same thing about labor. It lasted twenty-eight hours. The pain of each contraction was excruciating. I never did fully dilate. The monitors attached to both me and the baby displayed signs of near-fatal trauma. The doctor used every instrument imaginable to try to pull the baby from me. In the process,

part of my insides went, too.

The thought running through my mind during this ordeal was, "So this must be how God gets even with women who have abortions." It didn't help that Steven's face was displaying panic and fear.

Almost immediately after our baby was born, we noticed that the forceps had made deep indentations in our new daughter's head. "When will they go away?" we asked. The doctor explained that they might never disappear. The pediatrician agreed. We were saddened, yet grateful that she was alive. As a matter of fact, I was grateful to be alive myself.

We wrestled with names for several days and finally settled on Kalla Paige. In my eyes, she was the most beautiful child ever born, and she always will be. There's something very special about birthing a baby and holding it in your arms after you've lost one – by choice or not.

And guess what? Steven agreed. He looked into Kalla's eyes and really *did* fall in love! On top of that, the indentations in her head went away miraculously – and very quickly.

● ● ●

I faced the responsibilities of being a wife and a mother in a completely run-down condition. It took weeks — even months — to recover from labor and childbirth. I walked through my full-time job each and every day almost unconscious.

"How am I going to keep my husband happy?" I asked. "Oh, God, how can I keep going?"

The demands and responsibilities kept piling up, and in addition, I began to feel a tremendous discomfort in my lungs.

I've always been susceptible to bronchitis, so I thought this may have been the onset of another bout with it.

The doctor gave me medication after medication, but nothing helped. I tried to go on, pushing myself to be the perfect employee, the perfect wife, the perfect mother.

And then, one night, I broke. My body just shut down. I ended up in the hospital, on oxygen, without the strength to move or speak. Steven and Kalla would come to visit me, and I'd just lay there. Not saying a word. And, all this time, we still didn't know what was wrong.

Three-year-old Kalla would peek through the bed rails and all the tubes that were attached to me and ask, "Can I sleep with you, Mommy? Are you coming home? Please come home with me, okay?" Those are tough questions when it suddenly appears that you don't have any options.

Steven told me later that Kalla wanted to sleep with him in our bed at night, and that she would scratch the sheets with her fingernails, trying to relieve the nervous tension until she could go to sleep.

The stress of being both Mom and Dad and working got to be too much for Steven, too, so he finally called my parents and asked them to stay at our house for a few days. The evening that they arrived, he ordered a huge pizza, carried it up to our bedroom, locked the door, and ate the whole thing.

The doctors (by now I had more than one, all specialists) continued to order all kinds of tests — X-rays, blood tests, scans.

I was all alone in my room one night during that long hospital stay when the doctor in charge of my case came to see me. "Is your husband still here?" he wanted to know.

"No," I answered. "He's pretty tired, taking care of the house and Kalla and his work, and then coming here to see me."

The doctor hesitated. "I want to run another test in the morning, and you may want him to be here for it." There was a concerned look on his face.

"What is it?"

"We're going to put a special scope down into your lungs to check out something we found."

I was stunned. I asked again, "What is it?"

"One of your X-rays showed a spot on your lung. Karla, have you ever smoked cigarettes?"

"Yes, but I quit years ago. Why?" I was terrified to ask the next question, but I had to know. "Is it cancer."

"I'm not ruling that out. We won't know until we take a closer look."

I didn't know what to say. So I said nothing. The doctor paused for a moment. "Should I call your husband?" he asked.

"No. I just want to be alone."

The doctor said good night, and left me. Really alone. Alone in the dark. Alone, mostly, to cry. To collect my thoughts and try to regain some of my strength to face the next day. I didn't understand what was happening to me. I thought that I was finally happy. Finally in love again. I had a beautiful child who loved me. So why this? Why now?

And again I cried out to God. "OH, GOD! THIS IS TOO MUCH! WHAT DO YOU WANT FROM ME, ANYWAY? HOW MUCH MORE CAN I TAKE?"

I was seriously angry. I ranted against God. I wanted to punch Him one.

It wasn't my voice doing the yelling. It was my soul. The deepest part of my being. And suddenly — it's so difficult to explain — suddenly, I connected. When I had expelled every inner thought, every guilty feeling, every angry thought, and finally reached a point far below the bottom, I connected with Him.

In an instant, I went from anger to peace. To silence, to a sweetness. I reached out to Him with my heart. In the midst of my pain.

It wasn't that He said anything. I just knew He was there. I felt a forgiveness and a love that brought me to tears...a wonderful kind of tears. My whole past was cleansed. Yesterday didn't matter. Nor did the uncertainty of tomorrow. I was bathed in a supernatural love. I experienced a peace that defies all reason — that surpasses my understanding. My God was truly with me!

I prayed, "Thank you, Lord, for being with me tonight. Thank you for loving me and forgiving me. Thank you for hearing me."

And I drifted off to sleep, comforted by the lullaby of God's Awesome Love.

— — —

Steven was at my side early the next morning when I went down for my test. They discovered that my lungs were filled with fluid, and they pumped out what seemed like quarts of it. There was no cancer. "Thank God!" I said it, and I meant it!

My smile told the whole story!

I didn't tell Steven about the previous night right away. I needed time to think about it and to absorb it. But I knew one thing: I finally discovered who Jesus is. He came to life in my life in Room 207 at Methodist Hospital in Minneapolis, Minnesota.

Options for the Future

God doesn't make any robots. He makes each of us with a free will. And He gives us choices. It's up to us to look at them, think about them, maybe even pray about them, and then choose.

You may be facing many difficult decisions in your life right now. And you're not looking for the *opinions* of your family, your friends, the media, popular culture, professional counselors, or people who write books. You may not even be seeking *answers* just yet. But you may be exploring your options. What choices do you really have? What have others chosen?

I can look back now and ask, "What options should I have considered? What paths should I have followed?" Which path would you choose?

Think about marriage. Should you marry someone if you're not sure you can commit yourself totally to that man? Marriage, I've discovered, is a major commitment. I believe we are to love our husbands more than ourselves. They are to love us more than themselves. It goes both ways. There are tremendous rewards in loving that way. It strengthens your relationship. But you have to be willing to take the first step. If you can't do that — and he can't do it — should you be getting married?

We all, by nature, want our own way. But if two people in a marriage each want their own way, they pull in opposite directions, and eventually they pull apart from each other. Are you willing to pull together — and give to each other — every day, day after day, year after year?

If not, then maybe your best option would be to wait until you can. Until you find that person you can love unconditionally.

There were conditions attached to my relationship with Pat. I had pledged my love to a dead man. It was easier to love Gary, because he had, through death, become perfect in my eyes. But what did I gain? Nothing.

Before you get married, even to someone you're sure is the right man, you may want to consider seeing a counselor. Not for the counselor's opinions — but for a better idea of who you are and who your future spouse is. This is simply another option you have. If you learn through counseling that you don't want to marry him, or discover that he doesn't really want to marry you, you haven't lost a thing. You've gained. You're not less of a person, you're a far better person.

There's something especially painful that some of you face every day. And that's an abusive relationship. My years in that kind of relationship were among my most difficult.

So, how do you deal with it? I'm not automatically suggesting the "divorce fix." There may be other options. Move out for a short time, until your spouse agrees to seek help. Move in with your parents or siblings if you have to. Find a shelter if you must. There are often helping hands and hearts as close as your yellow pages or a nearby church. If you run into a closed door, don't give up. Keep knocking until one is opened for you.

If you are abused, chances are it's not your fault. Maybe it isn't even his fault. It could be alcohol or drugs. Or unresolved anger. Or his upbringing — because I've read that one out of every three people who grow up in an abusive home becomes

an abuser later. It could be any number of things. The point isn't to pin the blame on someone or something. It's to get help before it's too late.

Whatever you decide to do, don't endanger yourself or the lives of your children. And don't withdraw into a small world of isolation and denial. Don't remain silent about it. Find *someone* to talk to. Start with God.

If you find yourself hungry for hugs — starved for affection — stop long enough to think about the future you could lose simply by hopping into bed with the first warm body you find. I thought Tom was the answer to my loneliness — he turned out to be an option that didn't fit my real needs. Actions have consequences. Did I really need a hug so desperately that I was willing to give up a child no one was prepared to have? I dis-

covered — the hard way — that a brief moment of "pleasure" isn't worth the pain that could follow. My decisions affect my life. And I'm the only one who can choose.

If you're faced with an unplanned or unwanted pregnancy, please don't put the blinders on. Take the time to look into other options — find other people who can help you. For starters, try to find a Christian counseling center. Look in the yellow pages. Try "Crisis Counseling." There's a center in almost every city — often more than one — and many of them charge little or nothing for their services. If they can't help you directly, they'll readily point you to someone who can. You really *do* have the time to check into these options. You don't have to rush into anything. Take a deep breath before you jump. Remember that! It's important!

My abortion was my last stop on a long list that included a death, denial, and abuse. It was a symptom of what I believe I had become — someone who had little time for God, and who honestly believed I was strong enough to fix everything on my own.

Not everyone who has had an abortion has had the regrets or experienced the guilt and the pain of separation that I did. For whatever their reasons, many women are comfortable with their decisions. And as I said at the beginning, it's not my position — or anyone else's — to sit and judge. None of us can see inside another person's heart or mind.

I only wish that someone had told me there are other options. Of course, the two obvious ones we all can easily think of are:

Have the baby and live with your decision.

Have an abortion and go on with life. (And live with your decision.)

It may require a lot of discussion, a lot of planning, a lot of rearrangement of priorities and schedules, but the options are out there:

You could have the baby and let a loving family adopt him or her.

You could, like my friend Michelle, have the baby, bond with it, and keep it. (I often wonder if her story is an accident, or if there's something divine going on in her life.)

You could, perhaps, tell you parents or sister or brother about your pregnancy, and live with them for the first few years to ease the financial strain and allow you to get on your feet again.

This is a really difficult one, but your parents or a sibling might

choose to raise the child as their own...or jointly raise your child with you. In this case, I do believe you will have to tell the child the whole story at an early age. Kids should never be placed at risk of finding out the truth from someone other than you.

I know a young woman who had her baby, and then met her husband when her son was almost three years old. The wonderful thing is, he loves the son as if the boy were his own. And the feeling is mutual. Now, they have another son together.

Another friend of mine met a married man, fell in love, got pregnant, and was then left on her own to raise her son. She has never gotten married, he is now nearing high school graduation, and mother and son are happy, complete, and content together. He's a great kid, too!

The people I've met have stories as varied as life itself.

One couple discovered, through medical tests, that their child-to-be would likely have Down's Syndrome. They were confronted with nagging doubt and total fear. Yet they ultimately chose to have their baby, and they haven't regretted that decision for a moment. That special child has brought special blessings to their lives.

If you're reading my words and a friend, or sister, or daughter is facing this issue, do the loving thing. Don't judge. Please just share the options. Give of your time. And care enough to ask the tough questions. "Why are you thinking about doing this?" "How will you gain?" "In what ways might you lose?" "What is your plan?"

Encourage them to talk it through. Help them answer these questions. If possible, encourage them to pray it through. Then simply love them.

There is one other area of life in which you have many options. And that's the matter of faith. And I'm not talking here about ritual, or even religion.

I've been very candid in this book about how I came to have a strong and meaningful relationship with God. I finally realize how important it is. Jesus, I believe, died out of love. Love for me. No one else ever did. Not Gary. Not Pat or Jim or Tom. Not even Steven.

I've finally discovered that when I face a challenging issue in my life — or a problem that's too tough for me to handle — I have God to turn to. In fact, when the phone rings, it usually interrupts one of my conversations with Him!

I've also discovered that I actually enjoy reading the Bible. No, not some stuffy old book from ancient times. I really enjoy

the new versions, like *The Message*. There's so much wisdom that applies to my life today. I have gained so much strength from it.

As meaningful as the Bible has become to me, it was of much greater importance to meet the Author. To experience His forgiveness. His love and His compassion. I honestly believe nothing in life is more important than that.

Your Next Step

The story you have just read was recently told to an audience of nearly 2,000 people in the form of a drama. The actors on stage were not professionals, but as they went through the lines and actions, I stood in the shadows off to one side of the stage and watched.

It all seemed so real to me at that moment. It was as if I was reliving the pain and anguish of each chapter of my life. Little did I know that there were others in the audience who were reliving their own pain.

At the end of the drama, I walked to the center of the stage and told a misty-eyed audience that, yes, that was my life. But,

I added, there is healing available to everyone. No human being has to live with guilt for anything they have ever done. God took care of that once and for all.

Some time ago, I read these words in *The Message:* "Those who enter into Christ's being-here-for-us no longer have to live under a continuous low-lying black cloud. A new power is in operation. The Spirit of life in Christ, like a strong wind, has magnificently cleared the air, freeing you from a fated lifetime of brutal tyranny at the hands of sin and death."

Those words mean a lot to me, because I was living under the black cloud of my abortion. I needed to have the air cleared. I needed to forget the tyranny of abuse, and get on with a whole life.

A few days after the drama was presented, I got a phone

call from a young woman who had been in the audience. She asked if we could get together to talk, and I said that would be fine.

When I answered my door later that afternoon, I could tell that she had something serious on her mind. We went to a room away from the rest of the family, shut the door, and I invited her to share her thoughts with me.

Almost immediately, she began to cry.

"I...I...just don't know what to do."

I took her hand and urged her to continue.

"I saw the play about your life...about your abortion...and about how you found freedom from guilt. I don't have that freedom at all. Not even close. I recently had an abortion, and all I've felt since is terrible guilt. It nags at me day and night. I can't

even sleep most of the time. It hurts so bad."

By now, we were both crying. I could identify with her.

We talked for a couple of hours that day, and talked more in the days that followed. Later, I learned from a friend that she had seriously considered taking her own life. The pain was so deep.

I'm nowhere near an expert on religion, so I didn't have answers to all of her questions. But I tried to explain that it wasn't religion that made the difference to me. Lots of religious people still feel guilty about things they've done. What made a difference to me was finding a real, personal, vital relationship with the one who created me inside my mother's womb. I discovered that relationship in a person named Jesus Christ, who, it says in the Bible, "personally took on the human condition, and

entered the disordered mess of struggling humanity in order to set it right once and for all." And that is what I needed most.

I don't know what your personal situation is. You may or may not have had an abortion. You may or may not be feeling guilt or remorse. Please understand that I'm not saying you have to think certain thoughts or feel a certain way. But perhaps there are other things that are preventing you from enjoying a whole and joyful life.

A long time ago, Jesus said, "I came so they can have real and eternal life, more and better life than they ever dreamed of." I believe those words are truth.

I believe that you can have a better life than you ever dreamed of by inviting Jesus to come into your life. He'll forgive you of anything and everything that is giving you feelings of guilt and

pain. And He'll show you how to live the fullest life you can in the days ahead.

If you do that, and you follow the great plan for life that God has created for each of us, I promise that you will be a different person! Fresh! Brand new!

I wish I could sit down with you right now, and take your hand, and somehow encourage you to fully consider all of your many options.

If you are alone and lonely, don't leap into a relationship that you know isn't right for you. It is better to be lonely than trapped in misery.

If you are already in a relationship that has become abusive, get away to a safe place and get help. There are people who truly care.

If you are pregnant and considering an abortion, think about ways to protect the young life growing inside you. Perhaps some loving person is out there, waiting to love and care for your baby.

If you are living with guilt from an abortion you have already had, I believe the only way to heal is to let Jesus do the healing. Find out about the forgiveness and love and compassion God offers to everyone — especially you.

In every decision you face, please take a deep breath — pause for a moment before you decide. Make a list of all of your options, and consider them carefully.

Someone I admire greatly once said, "If you fall, remember to fall forward!" And I can add, "Don't look back!"

Epilogue

You may be wondering about my life today.

Steven and I enjoy our relationship every day. We are both willing to admit that the road is not always smooth. (Actually, sometimes, he's impossible!) Every marriage faces challenges, and ours is certainly no exception. But because we both seek to follow the path that God offers to us, we believe we can grow in our love for each other, and keep our commitment strong.

As we sat across the table from each other to work on this book, I had to relive all of my past experiences. And somehow it's brought us closer together. Honesty and openness really *do* matter.

Kalla is now in elementary school, and she's active in all the things kids enjoy. She's an "outdoor" person (like her mom and dad) and enjoys biking, in-line skating, swimming, Girl Scouts, and creating elaborate chalk drawings on our driveway. She is doing well in school, too, and we are very proud of her.

I now have a job I truly love! I work for a cemetery, and help families who have lost a loved one make their arrangements. In my business, it's called "Family Service," and I do feel as though I'm being of service to families at their time of greatest need. And every time I have to help a family bury their baby, I think about my baby. The one who had no funeral. Who had no burial. Who has no grave marker with her name on it. Yes, I do cry a lot on the job.

There isn't a week that goes by that I don't think of my

"baby who could have been." I think how wonderful it would be for Kalla to have an older sister (or brother), and how much she or he would enjoy Kalla — with her little tricks and jokes and riddles.

I really do believe that our family will one day be complete — that there is a place called heaven. I know the first thing I'm going to do when I get there is hold my baby, shower her with hugs and kisses, and experience all those hugs and kisses I've missed out on!

AN INVITATION TO MY READERS...

I want to help you deal with the challenges in your life in any way I can. I know you may be facing tough choices, and may not be aware of all the options you have. I may be able to help — if not, I will try to direct you to someone who can.

If you decide you want to write to me, I'll do my best to answer you. And I'll keep your letter confidential. You can write to me even if there's just something you want to get off your mind. Here's my address:

Karla Gottry
c/o Priority Multimedia
Box 41540
Mesa, Arizona 85274-1540

MULTIPLE COPY ORDER FORM

If you bought this book in a bookstore, you have done something very special for others. You have helped make it possible for non-profit organizations — those dedicated to helping women in crisis — to purchase this book at a lower cost, to give to those women free of charge.

Bulk copies are available to non-profit organizations at a significant discount off the cover price.

25 copies (minimum)	$2.50 each —	$62.50
26 to 50 copies	$2.25 each	
51 to 100 copies	$2.05 each	
101 to 500 copies	$1.90 each	
501 or more copies	$1.80 each	

Please add $12.00 shipping & handling charge for each order, regardless of quantity ordered.

Total Number of Books _____ X Price _____ = $ _____
Plus shipping/handling charge $ 12.00 _____
Minnesota non-exempt buyers must add sales tax* $ _____
Total $ _____

* Exempt buyers must include exemption certificate with order

Name _____

Title _____

Organization _____

Street Address _____

City _____ State _____ Zip _____

Phone/Fax _____

E-Mail _____

Mail to:

Macalester Park Publishing Company
7317 Cahill Road, Suite 201
Minneapolis, MN 55439

Or call: (612) 941-6830
Fax: (612) 941-3010

For information on other products from Priority Multimedia, please send a self-addressed, stamped envelope to:

Priority Multimedia Group, Inc.
P.O. Box 41540
Mesa, AZ 85274-1540

Information is also available on the World Wide Web at:

http://www.prioritymm.com

Karla's e-mail address is:

karla@prioritymm.com